A Story of Two
Third Grade Classes

UNITED STATES of FRIENDSHIP

Pen Pals of 9/11

Elaine L. Mroczka

VIA AIR MAIL
PAR AVION

Julie O'Connor, Ph.D.

VIA AIR MAIL
PAR AVION

Fulton Books
Meadville, PA

Published by Fulton Books 2022

ISBN 978-1-63985-118-8 (paperback)
ISBN 978-1-63985-119-5 (digital)

Cover Design by Alex Perla, Elaine L. Mroczka and Julie O'Connor, Ph.D.

Printed in the United States of America

Acknowledgement

This book is dedicated to the people who lost their lives on September 11, 2001, and to all their families and friends, forever changed on that tragic day. We also are grateful to the first responders who risked their lives to save others in need. We have not forgotten you. Lastly, we devote this book to the children, growing up in uncertain times, finding resilience, being kind, and building a hopeful future!

T uesday, September 11, 2001, began as so many other days did in my many years of teaching! During my commute to school that morning, I recall the cloudless azure blue sky and the bright sunshine on that morning. It was a beautiful, crystal-clear late summer day! There was a crispness in the air that signaled fall wasn't far off!

September in Illinois

After the fact, all the memories of that morning became seared in my mind. I remember it was absolutely gorgeous weather as I rode on the bus across the George Washington Bridge from New Jersey to my job at PS 48 in New York City. The sky was clear, and I could see all the way downtown from the top of Manhattan as I crossed the Hudson River.

George Washington Bridge, New York City

Our morning, my third grade class at Circle Center School in Yorkville, Illinois, began with the usual routines. That morning, we had our library/computer period. Half of my twenty-six students were perusing the library for a good book to check out and read. The other half of the class was in the computer lab, learning some basics of use. Suddenly, another teacher rushed into the library, telling both the librarian and me that a parent had come to school, stating that "the country was under attack!" Planes had been deliberately flown into buildings in several places in our country!

Circle Center School, Yorkville, Illinois

I was teaching my third grade class when a teacher came in saying that someone flew a plane into the World Trade Center. We thought it was a small plane and that a pilot had done it by mistake. I continued teaching, and I received a message from a person from the office who called my classroom phone. The message was from my sister-in-law in California who was letting me know that my husband who worked in New York City was safe. I was thoroughly confused. Then another teacher told me that the situation was very bad. Now it was two planes. We were starting to panic.

What I later learned was that my husband could not reach me by cell phone because of the cell towers being taken out downtown and the sheer volume of calls being made. He was able to reach my sister-in-law in California who was able to call my school in New York City from her landline phone.

I remember trying to conceal the shock and horror I was feeling until we received a directive from the principal and the district superintendent as to how we were to address this news with the children in our classrooms. Our school's open house was scheduled for that week, where our parents come in the evening to meet their child's teacher, see their child's classroom, and view examples of their child's work. This was promptly cancelled and rescheduled for a later date. We were instructed to tell our students the basic facts of what had happened in three locations in our country that morning. Having been in our classrooms all day, with no access to any media for the most part, of course, we also didn't know what or why this was happening. We honestly told our students that we were all in shock too.

Slowly, but surely, parents started to pick up their children. They wanted to be with their kids. When the last few children were left, I was told I could go home. With the George Washington Bridge as well as all public transportation being halted, I began a trek filled with hitchhiking and depending on the kindness of strangers to get to my front door in New Jersey.

When traveling home, I looked up to see the type of army helicopters that you see in war movies, with propellers making a deafening sound. By then, we had learned about the Pentagon and Pennsylvania, and we were not sure that the threat was over for the day. I was aware we were in an active wartime defense mode, and it was terrifying.

Of course, the students, their families, and I were all glued to our TV sets that evening. Everyone was in total disbelief that this kind of evil existed in our world! The next day, this crisis was what was on everyone's minds. No child could focus on their class work but were consumed with the horrific events from the previous day. The children were filled with questions and concerns that were very difficult to answer and discuss. We talked about feelings that we were having, as well as other children, most likely in New York, and what they must be feeling. The topic of "needing to do something to help" kept surfacing in these discussions.

That evening, I thought about the children in my class. Whose parents worked in the World Trade Center? Which stranger on the bus from that morning was in that building? So many people died, and I could only imagine how great a loss was about to be realized throughout the entire tristate area. I was grateful to have my sister and husband home after their own harrowing journeys from Manhattan.

Now eight- and nine-year-old third graders were limited in what they are able to do to help, but we could "reach out" to other children who possibly were closer to this tragedy and were more affected by these events. Our only purpose was to let these children know that "others cared" about them! It really didn't matter that we knew no one that had been affected directly by this tragedy. We just knew that fellow Americans were hurting.

Teaching third graders after such a shocking tragedy is something for which I was not prepared. One of my students lost her cousin in the attack. There were also ongoing fears we were dealing with, such as how we could get from one area of the city to another, because nobody wanted to take public transportation. Security changes made things completely different in our daily lives. Yet, while we felt alone having our own city attacked, we were also aware of the sympathies expressed by others across the country, and it felt comforting.

Thus, my class embarked on a pen pal letter writing activity! The children wrote, "Dear Third Grader," and introduced themselves. They shared their feelings of concern, sympathy, and fear about what had happened. They also shared interesting facts about themselves, their likes, their pets, and their families. I, too, wrote a letter to a "Third Grade Teacher," along with a class list of my students, expressing our sincere sympathy for what they'd experienced. I packaged up the letters, and addressed the envelope to:

> Any Third Grade Class
> Any Elementary School
> New York City, New York

A lady at the Yorkville post office suggested a Broadway Street zip code, which I added to the envelope! And off it went in the mail!

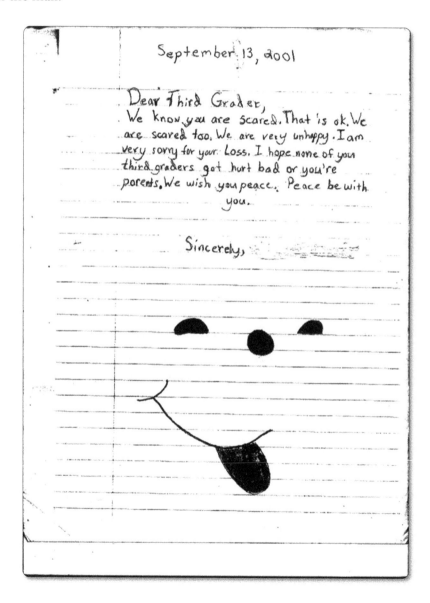

I was really taken aback when I received a large envelope of letters addressed to "Any Third Grade Class." I was deeply touched and knew that my students had to return this kindness by responding. New Yorkers have a reputation for being tough and gruff, so to speak. However, I excitedly tore open the letters, not acting "cool" at all! I handed out the letters at random, and my students were instantly motivated to learn about this far off community of rural Illinois.

I had no idea if those letters would be delivered or if they'd reach a class of third graders, and I explained that to my class. But at least we had the knowledge that we tried to help other children through their grief, and that was a reward in itself! After that, we tried to return to some normalcy in our classroom, filling our days with the usual routines, which was a difficult task under the circumstances.

We started our process of responding to these special letters. My students wrote about their hobbies, what they were learning, and their pets. I remember one of my students reading about her pen pal's horse, which was unheard of in my class's urban neighborhood! The children included drawings and wrote their feelings about 9/11. By writing back to their peers, they felt safer to admit their fears and insecurities.

From a teacher's perspective, I was so happy to see my students engaged with writing. They were excited to revise and rewrite until they produced a final copy ready to send back to their new friends. The multicultural connections also excited me as an educator. Many of the students in my school were first generation Dominican and spoke Spanish at home. I was excited for them to learn about the Midwest, such a different US culture.

Finally one day, a package arrived for "Mrs. Mroczka's Third Grade Class" from Mrs. Julie O'Connor's Third Grade Class at PS 48 in New York City! What a day that was! We were ecstatic that our letters had been delivered to a class of third graders, and they'd responded! Her students' letters were filled with emotions that typically aren't expressed in a classroom setting. Mrs. O'Connor's students were so touched that children some 850 miles away, in a rural town in the Midwest part of the country, cared about them! Thus began a pen pal project that was carried on throughout the remainder of the school year. Geography, letter writing skills, and proper grammar were just some of the skills that improved with this activity, not to mention the "life lessons" that were learned from being kind to other people whom we really didn't know but must have been grieving.

Unbeknownst to us, our pen pal project picked up momentum like a snowball rolling down a hill! It kept growing bigger and bigger! About two months later, in early November, I received a note from the school secretary that Abby Goodnough from the *New York Times* had called me and wanted me to return her call. I figured that no one at the *Times* would even know me, let alone want to talk to me, so I thought someone was "pulling a practical joke on me!" But just to be on the safe side, I returned the call, saying I'd be available after the children left for the day. Shortly after, Abby called again! She was an educational reporter with the *Times* and had heard about our class writing letters to Mrs. O'Connor's class. Abby wrote an article about our pen pal project reaching out to children in New York City and published an article about it on November 19, 2001. Of course, my students were touched that their "acts of kindness" were receiving such recognition.

Being featured in a *New York Times* story was not something that I ever expected! I tried, mostly in vain, to explain to my third graders that this attention was truly a big deal. However, they did get excited by the next adventure in our story.

But our story doesn't end there! It seems a producer at the *Today Show* read the article in the *Times* and felt it was worthy of a spot on their show! So he had the NBC affiliate in Chicago come out to my classroom while the NBC crews in New York City went to Mrs. O'Connor's classroom. Both classes were filmed on Wednesday, November 21, 2001.

What an exciting day that was! Our children shared their letters, feelings, and expressions of thoughtfulness with a television audience. Our "Five Minutes of Fame" was broadcast on the *Today Show* on Tuesday, November 27, 2001. Of course, our class was watching the broadcast! So was everyone else that we knew! Our local paper, the *Aurora Beacon News*, picked up our story, and they, too, printed an article about us—this time on the front page! We also received many congratulatory notes and tokens of appreciation from strangers who had heard about our story!

The *Today Show* camera crew came to our school for hours, filming the students and interviewing a few of us individually. Their newfound fame was pretty awesome and actually was a bright spot in an otherwise dark time.

When the show aired, we were able to spot a few of the pen pals, matching some of the interview clips with their names. It was before social media, so that news story was the first time we saw what each other looked like! I was proud of how eloquent my students were. But what really amazed all of us was the process of creating a news program—how much the TV crew filmed, and how much gets cut! Even though they were there for hours, it ended up being a few minutes' story!

However, the show did a wonderful job at showing both of our environments and both of our classes—two different communities brought together by the empathy and compassion we were shown by Mrs. Mrozeka's class.

As our school year progressed, we continued marking each holiday with letters, candy treats, and pictures that the children had drawn, sending them back and forth to each other's classrooms. Then as our school year drew to a close, my husband, Tom, and I planned a trip to New York City in June of 2002 to finally meet Mrs. O'Connor and her students. I hand-delivered letters and little stuffed bears for each of her children from my students. That visit solidified my friendship with Julie. She and her husband, Jack, were gracious hosts while we were in New York. They spent time with us and shared with us a list of the "must-see and do" activities while we were there.

Elaine visiting New York City in June 2002

Our students were not the only ones to get a cross-cultural education with this project! We teachers got in on the excitement. When Elaine and her husband came to New York, she got to visit my school, and she received an official NYPD lapel pin from my school principal, whose many family members were police officers. It felt great to meet her in person and show her our appreciation.

Elaine visiting Julie's school, P.S. 48 in New York City

Later in August of 2002, when we were beginning our new school year here in Yorkville, Jack and Julie O'Connor came to Illinois to meet my children, now fourth graders. We had a fun pizza party after school one day so my former students could stay to meet Julie and share stories from her students, their pen pals. Again, this gathering made the local paper, the *Kendall County Record*, on the front page, on August 29, 2002.

Reprinted with permission of the Record Newspapers / Shaw Media

New York schoolteacher Julie O'Connor talks to Elaine Mrosczka's students at Circle Center Tuesday. (Record Photo by Tony Scott)

Thank you from New York
Big Apple teacher visits Circle Center class to thank students for their letters

By Tony Scott

Pen pal programs are fairly common.

But when Elaine Mroczka's third grade students at Circle Center Intermediate School in Yorkville began writing Julie O'Connor's third grade class at P.S. 48 Michael J. Buzcek School in New York last year, it was prompted by something many Americans weren't even thinking about on Sept. 10, 2001.

Shortly after the terrorist attacks on New York and the Pentagon last Sept. 11, Mroczka's class sent a package of letters to "Any Third Grade Classroom, Any Elementary School, New York, U.S.A.," and hoped someone would write them back.

The students heard back from O'Connor's class, and the two classes continued to write to each other throughout the school year. When the kids went home on summer vacation, some got home addresses and e-mail addresses and kept up with their newfound pen pals.

O'Connor visited Mroczka's kids, now fourth grade students, Tuesday at Circle Center. The visit gave them a chance to meet O'Connor, who brought along photos of her students.

Mroczka visited O'Connor's classroom in June. Mroczka noted that after the students' pen pal experience, she felt like she knew the New York students personally.

"I felt so close to them," she said.

O'Connor recalled the emotional moment when her class got their first in a series of special deliveries from Mroczka's class.

"When I opened up that first packet of letters, it was so touching, my principal and I were almost crying," O'Connor said.

The 27-year-old teacher said the letters meant a lot to her students.

"I always teach my students to care for others," O'Connor said. "They were on the receiving end of that, and they realized how good that made them feel. That was the best lesson."

The letters the New York students wrote to Illinois were cathartic in a way, allowing the children to show emotions they usually wouldn't express in a classroom setting, O'Connor said. Although none of the children lost parents in the tragedy, two of her students lost family members.

"When they were writing to their pen pals, it was a safe outlet for them to express what they really were feeling," she explained.

O'Connor looked at some of the pictures the children were sending to their Illinois friends, and she said they also helped her understand her students' feelings.

"I remember one little girl drew the twin towers with a sun and the sun had a sad face in it," she said. "That's very communicative, and I didn't know the girl was feeling that way."

O'Connor said not only was the experience helpful as an assignment that taught her students to write, but they began writing the letters on their own.

"If there was any free time, they would ask if they could write to their pen pals," she said.

The experience not only created a bridge between the students, but a friendship between the two teachers as well. O'Connor said the letters helped the students get something positive out of a tragedy, allowing them to reflect upon Sept. 11, 2001 not with a sense of loss but the feeling that good people do exist in the world.

"The second anyone tells them, 'What do you think of Sept. 11?,' I really think the next thing they'll say is, 'People really cared and reached out for me,'" she said.

My husband and I drove to Illinois that summer, and due to the different start dates of the school year in the Midwest, Elaine was able to get most of her students back in August to meet me! I wanted to express my gratitude, as well as the appreciation of my students, to this extraordinary teacher and these special students. They had reached out to us in September 2001 and continued our relationship throughout the entire school year. Their actions made us feel less alone. We knew that the rest of our country had our back. We felt a strong sense of unity, and I was grateful to them all.

Elaine and Julie

Some months later, I received a call, this time from a producer at Harpo Studios, Oprah Winfrey's company, at that time in Chicago. It seemed they'd heard of the unusual way Julie and I, along with our students, had become friends. Oprah was planning a show about friendships that began under strange circumstances. They requested that I send all of the information, copies of the newspaper articles, pictures, etc. to the producer for consideration. In the end, our friendship wasn't "unusual enough" to be used on Oprah's talk show, but they at least considered it!

On September 11, 2021, we just commemorated the twentieth anniversary of 9/11, a day that won't be forgotten! Julie and I are still friends and keep in touch. I taught another four years and retired with thirty-seven years of teaching service. I have had the privilege to travel the world with my husband. We have honored many of the Americans who lost their lives that September day by traveling to many of the memorials/museums honoring them. The life lessons, both good and evil, that we all learned from that tragic experience will live on forever. Just a simple act of kindness, beginning with eight- and nine-year-olds, can bring joy to many people. We feel we touched and helped those children in Mrs. O'Connor's class. Her children reaching out to us certainly enhanced our lives. The *Today Show* and the newspaper articles, both in New York City and in Illinois, possibly have encouraged other people to reach out and "do something good" to help others! Like ripples on a pond, our little act of kindness spread far and wide! Possibly the world could be a better place because of our third graders' example!

9/11 Memorial in New York City today

The Freedom Tower, New York City

The 9/11 attacks were designed to induce fear and sew insecurity in people, but they did not succeed due to people like Elaine Mroczka and her class. As opposed to feeling helpless, they took action. Her class made us feel empowered through writing about our feelings and knowing that everything would be okay. We would rebound and come together as a country. I hope that our students now, as adults in their late twenties, continue those acts of kindness that they showed each other all those years ago.

Elaine visiting Julie's class, June 2002

Julie visiting Elaine's class, August 2002

Elaine's visit to Ground Zero, June 2002

Ground Zero, New York City, June 2002

The rock marking the spot where Flight 93 crashed in Shanksville, Pennsylvania

Elaine's visit to the Shanksville, Pennsylvania Memorial site in 2016

Our unity is our strength!

About the Co Author

Elaine L. Mroczka grew up in a large family in Central Illinois. She has several degrees, with the last being a master of science in education from the University of Illinois in Champaign, Illinois. Elaine has enjoyed a wonderful career, teaching mostly primary children for thirty-seven years. Her last twenty-four years of teaching was in third grade in Yorkville, Illinois, where she was named the Most Influential Educator and also was named in *Who's Who Among America's Teachers*. She is now retired, enjoying family, friends, golf, travel, and has become a published author. She and her husband reside in Northern Illinois.

About the Co Author

Julie O'Connor, PhD, has been a teacher and instructional supervisor for over twenty years in both the New York City and Cliffside Park, New Jersey, public school systems, the latter of which is where she currently teaches. She also serves as the Educational Director for the Animal Protection League of New Jersey. Specializing in English language learning, Dr. O'Connor obtained her PhD for studying how "humane education," pro-social learning that includes kindness to animals, improves student education. She received master's degrees from both Mercy College and the Bank Street College of Education and her PhD in education from Northcentral University. Dr. O'Connor serves on her town council and lives in Northern New Jersey with her husband, two children, and two dogs.

Having received empathy from students in Illinois, Dr. O'Connor's students showed their own compassion to others living through trauma. She considers one of her greatest achievements to be connecting her students during that same September 11, 2001–2002 school year with a fund-raising project for the animals in the war-torn Kabul Zoo, which was featured in the *Weekly Reader* magazine. Empowering youth to make a positive difference is one of Julie O'Connor's main goals in life.